AF574414

OOOMMMMMM...

To Lauren Croall. Thank you for your love, encouragement, support, and modeling skills. Here's to eating strawberries.

ACKNOWLEDGEMENTS

CARLTON FISHER

Your red pen is still handy even twenty plus years since I graduated high school. Thanks Dad!

Designed & Illustrated by
Mandy Lehman: @manmanstudios
Jill Cleary: @jillcleary

ISBN: 978-0-578-50947-1

COUCH YOGA

NETFLIX & NAMASTE

BY PAUL FISHER

ARE YOU STILL WATCHING?

CONTINUE WATCHING

BACK

START YOGA WITH A BINGE

AH, BINGE WATCHING!

Smart TVs, On-Demand, Netflix, and Hulu, to name a few, make America's new favorite pastime (i.e. - watching television) possible. We understand. There are so many great, bingeable entertainment options. Pick your poison: *The Crown, Gilmore Girls, Breaking Bad* are all worthy ways to make Saturday slip away.

THERE'S ONE PROBLEM: GUILT.

We feel it too. How does one not feel guilty when your tush is softening like a ripening avocado? You're not the average American: You don't watch five hours of TV each day. Remember, DENILE ain't just a river in Egypt. Your Netflix history speaks the truth. The first step is always admitting there is a problem. You're a binge watcher, like the rest of us, who likely needs a little more exercise.

EXERCISE: GUILT'S REMEDY.

Reaching the remote is hard enough let alone getting off the couch. The show you're watching is great, the plot is thickening. Season two, episode three of *The Crown* is captivating, and you need to know what Phil and Liz are gonna do next. Standing up for a needed run would send gout-like pains through your joints. Nonetheless, your butt, bones, and back feel the effects of chips, wine, and malaise. Exercise is the first course on the get fit menu. If only you could keep binge watching, and get toned on the couch. Last time you tried to run and watch an episode on your iPhone you ended up needing a rhinoplasty.

INTRODUCING *COUCH YOGA: NETFLIX & NAMASTE.*

This guide to some of Yoga's great poses is a life and joint saver. You'll get enviable abs and firm glutes without pausing Hulu. It's Downward Dog from the comfort of a chaise lounge! Do a pose while you watch a show. *Couch Yoga: Netflix & Namaste* highlights 15 poses of varying difficulty you can perform from the comfort of a couch. The poses, with improved names and descriptions on how to perform them, are accompanied by recommended TV show or movie pairings to serve up the perfect living room exercise guide. Plus, you can do these exercises between episode views, potato chip noshes, or beverage sips.

WASHBOARD ABS, RIPPLING LATS, AND BUNS OF STEEL ARE SOOO CLOSE.

Grab the yoga mat, if you've got one, a fave food or drink, and plop that heinie down on the divan. Hit power on the Roku, flip the page to a pose, pull up the queue, hit play, and start working that core. In no time you'll fall in love with a great way to stay fit and may even consider taking the next step: attending an actual class.

Table of Contents

A Yoga Story

I can't remember when I did my first yoga pose, but it was definitely next to my couch. If memory serves me correctly, I was binge watching *The Walking Dead, Breaking Bad,* or another addictive TV series that my girlfriend, now wife, recommended. My guilt was high. My body definitely needed a workout, but I wanted to keep watching Rick Grimes (i.e. - *The Walking Dead's* male lead) slay zombies. Lauren recommended trying a few yoga poses. There were Plank, Downward Dog, Boat, and many more you could do without leaving the comfort of your living room or even your couch. "Why not?!" I thought. While I didn't know much about yoga, I was willing to give it a shot. So, I let the Netflix roll and started to do a Downward Dog. "This yoga crap is a breeze," I thought without really knowing what I was doing. But, what was the harm of giving something new a shot in the privacy of my living room. Little did I know that my first Downward Dog would lead to other poses and eventually a newfound, enjoyable, if not really odd at times, form of exercise.

I mastered the basic poses on my couch quickly. Magic was happening in my abs, they definitely were looking more like Ryan Gosling's everyday, I daydreamed. "Why not try a couple of classes?" I thought. The 'real thing' couldn't be much harder than or too different from a standard gym workout, right? Wrong! My first class and a really weird subsequent class opened my mind to how great and extremely different yoga can be from other forms of exercise.

The first class, away from the couch, was harder than expected. "Don't you just lay there, breathe, and chant to some eight legged Indian god?" I irreverently asked my wife on the way to class. "There's a pose where we just stand on our mats imitating a tree, right?" Lauren laughed but also snuck a look of loving disapproval. She encouraged an open mind and said, "It's tougher than you think, but it's really relaxing."

While people arrived, unrolled their mats, and began to prepare for "practice," which still feels like a word that should be reserved for team sports, I noticed something. These people were fit! Some had eight pack chiseled abs, even Ryan Gosling would envy. You could drop full-grown coconuts on them from a 20-foot extension ladder, and the fruit would fling skyward like a 10 year old on a trampoline. After seeing this, I made sure my Dri-Fit tee sufficiently covered the jelly protecting my eight pack. Maybe yoga was the path to enlightenment and a beach body!

The path ain't easy, though. Within 30 minutes I saw how difficult becoming an advanced 'yogi' is. 'Practice' started with an instructor guiding us through some mind clearing, while we lay on our backs. Sounds a little lame or unnecessary, right? Au contraire. It was soothing! Plus, it prepared us for the ball busting challenge and quirkiness to come.

After a half dozen or more poses, my quads were feeling a little cramped, sweat was beading from my brow. I was in the middle of a pose I didn't know completely how to say or do and started thinking "This is harder than I thought." The instructor commanded us to hold poses longer and longer and keep repeating them over and over. It really burned! I never held poses this long on the couch. A small lake of sweat from my brow had accumulated at my feet. I must have lost two pounds, and there were still thirty minutes left! After thirty more minutes of lunges, planks, attempted headstands, and, finally, stretching, I made it.

In 90 minutes, I realized yoga is friggin' hard! It didn't help that my wife and I chose an intermediate / advanced class. The next day, my whole body was sore. But, it was a good sore. I felt like I accomplished something. My chest, legs, and abs ached no differently than when I did a tough weight workout in college. It was pleasing to find another form of exercise for the repertoire. The first class opened my eyes to the challenge of yoga. A future class would expose me to yoga's quirkiness.

Hollywood is great at mocking subjects that are a little weird. In the movies *Couples Retreat* and *Forgetting Sarah Marshall,* the writers make fun of handsy yoga instructors in a few scenes. As the saying goes, "It's funny because it's true." My wife and I not only witnessed yoga instructors getting pretty cosy with guests, but also experienced it ourselves. One time, we were massaged and serenaded. Pretty odd, right? Here's how it happened.

It all started pretty benignly. After 80 or so minutes of punishing poses and contortions, we were told to lie down on our mats. "Breath deeply," the instructor commanded. Our hastened hearts began to calm. The room was filled with dopamine and endorphins. That's when things got a little freaky.

The lights were off, and the shades were drawn. Our eyes were shut. We were in a dark yoga cave. In the cave with us were 30 other little yogis all laying on their mats. We looked like a bunch of toddlers napping in daycare. Our yoga instructor wandered the room giving us commands in a mildly seductive tone. It felt like we were being hypnotized. Nonetheless, we all felt safe. Plus, there's safety in numbers, right? Wrong!

Suddenly, I was attacked! Given my surprise, my mind quickly started churning. I wondered, "Who is touching me," and "Is this normal?" I didn't fear for my life. I just didn't know who it was. Maybe Lauren, my wife, decided to adjust my form because I was lying on my back and not performing corpse pose correctly. This, surely, would cease soon. But, it didn't.

My arms were gently rotated so my palms faced upwards. Lauren definitely wasn't the one helping me with my form. It had to be the instructor.

More than a moment had passed since the yoga instructor ceased speaking. I opened my eyes and snuck a look confirming my suspicion: the instructor had snuck up on me. She now was making sure I was laying on my back correctly. You'd think after 38 years of sleeping one would know how to lie down, but apparently I wasn't doing it in correct yoga fashion. She made a few adjustments to my shoulders, then, things got weirder.

"Ooooo laaaaaa caaaathaaahsahnah. Sheeeeebop haaaahtahsahnah," she gently crooned less than six inches from my face. "What the hell was happening? Isn't she a yoga instructor, not a member of the Rat Pack?" I wondered. "Doesn't she know my wife is literally two feet to my left?" With my best efforts at telepathy I warned, "You better not go too far! My wife'll mess your ass up if your hands 'explore' too much." She didn't. I started to smile to avoid the embarrassment of laughing; it was the only antidote for guttural childlike giggles building below. Then something unexpected happened: it felt a little soothing.

Being accosted was a little weird. Like many, I prefer my space. Knowing I was in a compromised position and resistance would require sitting up and flinging the instructor to the ground, I just laid back and allowed myself to be serenaded like a sorority sister. It wasn't all that bad and would make for a funny story.

My accosting ended as quickly as it started. The chanting stopped. One last firm but caring press of my shoulders to the mat signaled the end. The instructor floated away. I wondered if her leopardesque hunger had ceased or if other yogis would be "victims." If she did set her gaze on another target, who would it be? Would she attack my wife too? That would be a hoot. Lauren likes her space even more than I do. Then she did! She did the exact same thing to her! What are the odds, right?

Class ended and I couldn't wait to talk to Lauren. As we left the studio and walked to the car, I finally addressed the elephant in the room. "What the hell just happened?" I asked. Lauren giggled. "I have no idea!" "That was hilarious!" I said. "I knew she was coming after you! I also thought she might go a little too far and you were gonna have to cut a bitch." "Exactly!" Lauren offered.

We joke about the experience to this day. We also remind ourselves of what yoga is. Camaraderie is common in yoga. Instructors help improve your form routinely. We both appreciate that because it ensures we are working our muscles and stretching correctly. It's also a way to relax and expand your mind. My mind definitely was expanded. It all started with couch yoga.

Yoga is now an intermittent component of my workout regiment. I started on the couch doing basic poses while having a laugh. I've got a mat, a yoga towel, and have even done hot yoga. While I still don't have Ryan Gosling abs, can't do a handstand, and would prefer to avoid being molested by yoga instructors, yoga is something I enjoy. My guess is, you will too. Ease yourself into it in a safe place, like the couch, and maybe you'll find your way to a class like I did.

READY to POSE?

CORPSE

our name

RIGOR MORTIS

Are you new to yoga? If so, this pose is the perfect way to ease into 'practice'. You literally don't need to do a darn thing. Just keep laying on the couch, and watching television.

On second thought, you need to do something. Drop the bon bons! Practice deep breathing. Check your pulse once in a while, for problems or to make sure you aren't dead, and you've got it.

binge pairing

What comes to mind first when we say "Corpse?" Zombies! Perform Corpse while watching *Walking Dead* or *World War Z.*

our name

WE'RE NOT WORTHY!

Child pose: the perfect way to bury your head in a couch cushion and console oneself when the story line doesn't go your way. It's also yoga's go to pose when you need a break. Kneel on the floor, rest your tush on your heels, and bow your head and hands to the floor worshipping a higher power.

Let tears flow!

binge pairing

The Crown expects your full attention while you perform this pose. *Wayne's World* is another worthy accompaniment for this pose

PLANK

our name

WRIST BUSTER

Seeking those Ryan Gosling like abs we mentioned? Plank is the potion. Start at the top of a push up. Don't do the push up. Just stay there and hold it. If you want to make it a little easier, go down to your elbows.

Guess what the world record is for this pose? 8 hours, 1 minute! Avoid this exercise in the midst of a comedy binge. Your abs will not survive the laughter.

binge pairing

Watch land lovers be made to 'walk the plank' in movies such as *The Goonies* or *Pirates of the Caribbean.*

COBRA

our name

G.I. JOE'S NEMESIS

They say Cobra pose strengthens the spine and firms the buttocks. Nice! Who doesn't want a nice ass!? This pose also has been known to help one achieve enlightenment and bliss by awakening the kundalini.

Similar to many yoga pose names like Savasana, we don't really know what kundalini means. Google it if you must know. Maybe it's yoga gobbledygook meaning "tush toner"!

---

binge pairing

The obvious movie or television show to watch is *G.I. Joe*. The less obvious movie to watch with this one is *Dumb and Dumber*. You'll have to watch it to figure out the connection.

DOWNWARD DOG

our name
HEAD IN SAND

Make a triangle with the floor as the hypotenuse. Your butt should be straight up in the air. Hold it as long as you can. It's not as long as you think.

Rumor has it this position was invented by the dog in Cujo. *The dog would perform this pose to aid in the digestion of its victims. Yogis don't like to admit that.*

binge pairing

The obvious pairing is with dogs, right? There too many "dog" movies to count. One could spend weeks picking movies about dogs without making a dent in the genre. Just start with *Old Yeller* or *Bolt,* and explore.

WARRIOR 1

our name

HERCULE'S BOULDER

Now you're starting to get into some serious poses! Stand on the couch and do a lunge. Once steady, lift your hands over your head. Both elbows should be next to your ears. Pretend you are holding the weight of the world above you.

Imagine if you stop holding this pose the sky will literally fall to the ground crushing humanity. Be sure to read the special instructions on this move.

binge pairing

Similar to "Dog" movies, there are too many "Warrior" movies to name. Some perfect, modern day classics such as *Braveheart, Troy,* or *Gladiator* are perfect.

CHIPS

WARRIOR 2

our name

EN GUARD!

Start with Warrior I aka Hercule's Boulder. Drop the imaginary boulder. You've carried enough weight. Turn your arms into an elongated spear at shoulder level. Your jugular is the spear's midpoint. As in Warrior I, be sure your front knee is positioned over your ankle.

Now stare over your outstretched fingertips into the distance at some abstract object.

binge pairing

To quote Inigo Montoya in *A Princess Bride*, "Hello, my name is Inigo Montoya. You killed my father. Prepare to die! Enguard!" Watch it.

TODDLER'S POSE

our name

KIDS ARE BENDY

Channel your inner toddler and imagine your hips and bones are malleable like PlayDoh. Start with Downward Dog. Stick your leg up in the air and curl it behind the grounded leg. If your hip socket hasn't popped, you'll get a nice opening and stretch.

If the hip didn't make it, call for help. Bennett, my nephew, recommends building a fort with the couch cushions before performing this move.

binge pairing

Since you're acting like a monkey turn on any *Curious George* series, just as a toddler would. ENCOURAGEMENT!!

PIGEON

our name

PROSTHETIC HIP PREVENTER

Got IT Band troubles? This move is for you. Start with one leg "Indian Style." Put the other leg behind you as if you were doing a lunge. BE CAREFUL! No need to pull or tear your groin. Once you've settled in, lean forward. Try resting your forehead against your ankle.

Your IT band is singing "THANK YOU" right now. If you're lovin' it and want some shuteye, put your head on a pillow and get some Zs.

---

binge pairing

Check out *Valiant,* an animated film about a pigeon who joins the Royal Pigeon Homing Service in 1944.

CHAIR

our name

VAULTER'S VICTORY!

Stand on the couch. Put both feet together. If you need more support, keep them slightly apart. We don't want you to fall through the coffee table you didn't move before starting your practice. Raise both hands above your head and lower your tush.

How low can you go? If you look like a chair, you're doing all right. Keep your abs clenched.

binge pairing

If you have HBO, imagine you occupy the Iron Throne from *Game of Thrones*. Pursuit of it is worth the effort!

Start in Warrior II. Straighten your forward leg as if you are doing the splits. Create a triangle with the couch as its base and your legs its sides. Once comfortable, bend the torso sideways from the hips toward the front leg.

If you've got moxie, try holding your front foot for a yoga-tastic hamstring stretch. WuuuuuuSaaaahhhhh!!!!

Looking to watch a little love triangle while you triangle? No, not smut you sicko. Catch *While You Were Sleeping*.

BOW

our name

HUMAN DREIDEL

Start by awakening yourself from Corpse with a Cobra, thus lifting your chest from the floor. Next, curl your heels toward your head and grab your ankles. Hold it but don't snap your spine! The writers of Couch Yoga accept no liability for you breaking vertabrae.

This move ain't for the faint of heart. Legend has it great warriors would perform this pose while making their bows. They'd chant "Dhanvarasana, Dhanvarasana" repeatedly to channel their spirit into the bow thus becoming one with the weapon.

binge pairing

Watch *Brave* while doing this move. Don't like Animation? Watch *Hunger Games,* Katniss.

BRIDGE

our name

HUMAN HALF DOME

If you do this more than once, you're entering the world of yoga gods. Start in Corpse with both feet nearly against your glutes. Invert your hands on either side of the head so the fingers point toward the toes. In a coordinated movement between the torso, arms, and legs, thrust the pelvis skyward.

Your crotch will now be the apex of a human half dome. Letting someone sit on top of you is dumb. So, don't do it doofus.

---

binge pairing

Check out *Free Solo*. You'll see Alex Honnold scale the real Half Dome without a rope. If you aren't into rock climbing, just search "Yosemite" or "Half Dome" and you're bound to find a worthy documentary to put your mind in a Zen-like state.

z z z

BOAT

our name

SACRED FEMININE

You know the drill: We start with one pose and add something to it. This is the last time you'll start in Corpse. The idea is to make a V with your butt as its base and upper and lower bodies its sides. Lift the upper and lower body simultaneously with your waste as the pivot point.

If you can lift the glutes too you're a witch. Wingardium leviosa! Try and reach the arms around the calves. Don't fall into the couch.

binge pairing

Are you wondering why we named it 'Sacred Feminine'? Watch Tom Hanks in *The DaVinci Code* to find out why.

our name

BIG TREE FALL HARD

Stand on the couch. Lift one foot and press the arch against the knee or higher. If you are really flexible, you may be able to get it high into the inner thigh. Now just stand there and focus on using your abs to keep balance.

Whatever you do, make sure you fall on the couch if you lose your balance. Couch Yoga writers will not pay your medical bills or for new furniture if you fall through the coffee table.

binge pairing

Groot recommends *Guardians of The Galaxy*. Fantasy films aren't your thing? No worries, check out Dr. Seuss's *The Lorax*.

WHAT NOW?

Yoga can be easy, if you do it right. We know you'll become a super bendy, yoga master quickly. Plus, you'll eventually exhaust the bingeable media pairings and may even get sick of posing alone. "What now?!" you'll ask. Go to an actual yoga class!

When you step into the real playing field of Yoga, you'll want to be prepared. Nobody likes walking in blind lest you feel dumb. We can help. Here are some tips we've gathered from surveying hundreds of yogis. Well, actually, we asked less than ten. We stopped asking people for tips because everyone kept saying the same thing.

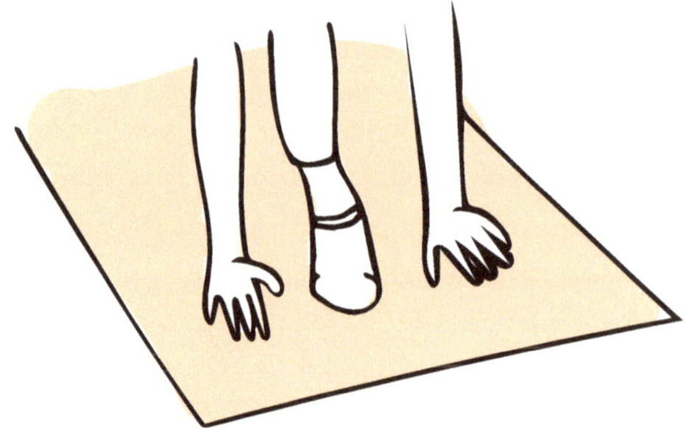

Get a Mat

Poses on a hard floor start to hurt. Most yoga classes are at least 60 minutes. Some even approach 90 minutes. Without a mat, your palms and feet will take all the punishment. For all the tough guys out there who may prefer to be closet yogis, getting a mat will out you. Regardless, your fingers and toes will love that you did even though your ego may not. Ignore any haters and just remember, you're gonna have chiseled abs. The haters will not.

Get a Yoga Towel

Get a yoga towel. "What the hell is a yoga towel?" you say. "Can't I just use a beach or regular towel?" Sure, you can use those too. A yoga towel is a little thinner, has little rubber grippies, and is of an ideal length and width to cover the yoga mat. You also might ask, "Why do I need a towel? Am I really going to sweat that much?" Yes. You will sweat THAT much. You'll be mid Warrior pose and start wondering when a faucet was installed on your body and who left it open. If you're doing Hot Yoga, the room temperature will approach 105 degrees F. Even in a regular yoga class, room temperatures can be 80 degrees F. Without a towel you'll feel like you're on a Slippin' Slide and will look like a horse on roller skates. People will laugh. Lakes of water will pool on the floor around you.

WEAR APPROPRIATE CLOTHING

Ladies, nobody wants to see your vajayjay, poonani, flower, lady garden, or whatever you call your privates. Dudes, nobody wants to see your cock, balls, weiner, shaft, johnson, family jewels, or whatever you call your privates. Abs, guns, quads, and some other muscles are ok to see. Keep what's supposed to be in the dark in the dark. Remember when Lululemon came out with see through yoga pants? They got crap for it.

PREPARE to BREATHE

You are going to breath as a group a few times. They are going to tell you to perform Ujjayi breath during "practice." At first it'll seem weird, but then you'll do it as a group and it'll be ok. I've heard some people describe it as lamaze breath. Ujjayi isn't lamaze. This technique helps one calm the mind and warm up the body with deep breathing techniques. In class it sounds like everyone is having a joint orgasm. It doesn't feel as good though.

DON'T FART

Nobody likes a stinker, especially in a sealed, heated room. So, go easy on the beans and other gut wrenching foods before class. No one really cares about how much you're trying to improve your micro biome. Do I need to explain more?

Maybe you're ready for more. You've mastered the basic, and some not so basic, moves on your couch. The abs are starting to take shape. (A four pack now exists where the belly was originally undefined, but you aren't quite at six pack level yet.) Watching the recommended bingeable content while you yoga may be getting boring. If you're daring enough, take the leap and sign up for a class at your local studio.

NAMASTE

Please take heed of the following precautions when performing couch yoga.

Always practice under the supervision of another adult 18 years of age or older.

Never perform couch yoga under the influence of drugs, alcohol, or other mind-altering substances.

Always check with your doctor before adding couch yoga to your workout routine.

Perform couch yoga free of any objects surrounding the couch. At least 10 feet of clearance between your couch practice space and any objects is recommended.

Never perform couch yoga with the couch on top of a trampoline or underneath a ceiling fan. Do we need to explain why? The results aren't pretty.

Perform couch yoga in an environment free of cats, dogs, rodents, and toddlers. Small dogs and squirrels tend to confuse some of the poses with items the encounter in the natural landscape. On occasion they have tried to climb the models or claim them as "territory." Those pesky little devils.

Perform couch yoga without the TV or smart device actually playing. These devices are notoriously distracting. While watching the boob tube, one can 'zone out' or be left in a hypnotic trance for extended periods of time. If you must have the TV a rollin' please only perform the following poses: Corpse, Childs, Cobra, Dog, Pigeon, Plank, Boat, and Bow. Performing any of the other poses outside of regularly scheduled breaks in the action is dangerous. Don't say we didn't warn you. We had the TV off during production and our highly trained models still had to maintain complete and total focus. Oftentimes they worried about landing head first on the floor. If you partake in the other moves we recommend installing braces in your walls to attach a harness to supplement your practice. Don't worry the wall hooks can be repurposed for pictures.

For maximum couch yoga safety and absorption of Vitamin D, locate the yoga couch and TV outside. Practice is safer when you are free of common household obstacles, such as wires, lamps, and coffee tables. Yogaing on top of rubber playground surfaces in a shaded location is ideal. You'll get less bumps and bruises and avoid skin cancer. You're welcome!

PAUL FISHER

Paul fashions himself as a tongue-in-cheek modern "Renaissance Man." He believes humor and health are two keys to living a happy life. When he isn't riding his bike, doing planks, or running, you can find him lounging on the couch binge-watching HBO GO, Hulu, or Netflix cracking snarky jokes with his wife. Paul believes heavy consumption of compelling TV is not only a great leisure activity, but also helpful in life. He has the ability to quote movies at will, regardless of how arcane the reference may seem.

CPSIA information can be obtained
at www.ICGtesting.com
Printed in the USA
LVHW070455051219
639507LV00018B/117/P

9 780578 509471